REAL ESTATE

INVESTING:

BEGINNERS GUIDE TO FLIPPING HOUSES,
WHOLESALING, INVESTMENT PROPERTIES,
COMMERCIAL REAL ESTATE, VACATION
RENTALS, PROPERTY MANAGEMENT,
VACATION RENTALS, LEASE OPTIONS AND,
REITS

By: Glenn Nora

Table of Contents

Introduction

While investing in real estate can most definitely help you to generate a lifetime of passive income, it is important to have the right expectations when you first get started if you want to succeed with real estate investing.

First, it is important to understand that it takes a lot of time and effort to create a passive income stream when it comes to investing in real estate.

In addition, it can be said that you will always have to be aware of your real estate investment and the maintenance of your property which means there is nothing passive about investing in real estate.

Likewise, doing the required research to find the right neighborhood and the right property within that neighborhood isn't something that is going to happen overnight, it is going to take serious dedication and planning before you start seeing traction in your chosen real estate investment.

In addition, you can always hire a management company to manage your real estate property but it also takes time and effort to hire a good management company and maintain a good working relationship with that company.

However, you will eventually get to a place where the amount of time and energy you have to put in on your real estate investment will be far less and you will begin to reap the profits of your real estate investment.

Thus, it is important to not lose faith when the going gets tough and to instead remember that successful real estate investment is like a marathon as opposed to a sprint which means that slow and steady wins the race.

This book was written for those soon-to-be real estate investors who are ready to get into the game and are looking for a sound entry-point. There are many different types of real estate investment methodologies, and in this book we're going to take a look at all of them. This book will also greatly benefit beginner real estate investors who are now realizing that they may be in a position to upgrade or purchase again. And despite all the warnings you'll hear about how hard it is to qualify these days, it's actually not as difficult as you may have thought.

Investing in rental real estate does not have to be a fulltime activity and you can do it in your free time. Anyway, you may come to enjoy it so much that you want to do it full time, but it is not necessary. In other words, you do not have to quit your day job to give real estate investing a try.

Chapter 1: Creating Passive Income with Real Estate

Passive income is slowly becoming a widely-used option as a source of employment. People often create passive income with goals such as paying off student loans, making extra spending money, and even having the ability to travel the world. Now to achieve this, there will still be start-up work and a lot of patience, as learning anything new can have its ups and down. Some options may even have start-up cost, but if done correctly it may potentially turn into ten times the income in a small amount of time. When deciding on what to invest your time in for a source of passive income, it is important to look at your goals.

You've finally purchased your first real estate property and you can now call yourself a real estate investor. But you are beginning to observe that you are constantly busy running your real estate business. You are either attending to one complaint from your tenant, or you're reminding them that their rent is due, and in between that you are still driving for dollars, or one contractor is delaying the supply of some material for you next fix-and-flip project. You have cash flow, but the hassles are getting too hectic and your team isn't as perfect as you thought. In fact, you are beginning to think the business is running you instead of you running the business!

Well, that's an indication that you need to take your real estate business to the next level; make your business passive! What would be the point of generating wealth if you cannot enjoy the time freedom that comes with more money? Wealth is supposed to give you the freedom to spend time with family, friends, and loved ones, learn new skills, and find other ways of multiplying your wealth and giving back to society. With more wealth, you should be able to have enough time to shift your attention to more important things in life aside from chasing money.

However, the reverse seems to be the case with a lot of real estate investors, as they are constantly on their toes and working their heads off. It really doesn't have to be so. Maybe in the initial stages, it should be expected. But after a considerable amount of time in the business, you should be able to lay back and watch cash pour into your account without backbreaking effort on your part.

Real Estate Partnerships

What if you have just one property and you still want passive income from real estate? What if you don't want to completely entrust the management of your property to a property manager, but still want to make your business passive? Here's what you can do: consider going into real estate partnerships.

Going into partnerships means that responsibilities are shared between the partners of the real estate business through an agreement. Finance distribution is not the only goal of real estate partnership; division of tasks such as taking turns in managing your properties, and joint decision making are also vital parts of partnerships. Depending on the partnership terms, each partner has their own responsibilities to fulfill without taking on the bulk of the duties of a one-man investment.

Look with a Plan

Starting the process of looking for a real estate investment property is exciting, so much so, that it can be easy to jump in without taking the time to ensure you know what it is you are getting yourself into. Likewise, just because real estate investment is recommended for every investor at one point or another, doesn't mean it is right for you, right now. Making a plan, first and foremost, will help you to ensure that it is really the optimum way for you to invest in the moment. When making your plan it is important that you take a hard look at your current situation while you go over the following details.

When it comes to determining a successful plan, the first thing you are going to need to do is to determine where you are currently at. This means going through all of your financial documents and determining exactly how much you have compared to how much you owe. This will be useful when it comes to anticipating what types of loans you get, while also helping you determine what it is that you can realistically afford.

Consider your support system

While having a reliable support system will make it easier to get into any type of investment for the first time, it is especially crucial when it comes to real estate investments. This is due to the fact that there is such a wide variety of variables that need to be taken into account on a regular basis, many of which you likely won't be anticipating your first time out of the gate. Knowing that you have someone available to bounce ideas off of alone will make the entire process less stressful and allow you to move forward with as much confidence as possible when it comes time to close your first deal.

Chapter 2: Getting Ready to Invest in Real Estate

Deciding what niche and strategy to use is one thing; getting your finances ready to actually start investing is another ball game altogether. Depending on your wealth stage, you may need to find some other means of saving enough money at least to cover initial expenses and make a down payment for the property you want to purchase.

Here are some tips on how to save or set aside some money for your real estate investment career.

- **Make savings a priority.** Realize that each time you spend money unnecessarily; you are going in opposition to your goal of saving enough money for your down payment. Let your money spending habits reflect the value you place on your goals.

- **Automate your saving process.** Open a separate savings account and give a standing order for a certain amount to be deducted from your monthly paycheck into the account.

- **Utilize all unexpected money.** Money does not come to you only through your monthly paycheck.

When you get cash gifts, tax returns, bonuses, etc., try to put all or most of this extra money into your savings account.

- **Build a side hustle.** There are a lot of ways you can use the extra hours when you are not working on your day job to create extra income. Freelancing, for example, is of the hundreds of ways to earn money on the side. Think up things that you are passionate about that can generate income without affecting your main source of income. And make sure the income from the side hustle goes towards your down payment.

Building a Team

Does it not make sense to have a team made up of professionals who will bring their knowledge to bear in making your investing career a success? One way or another, you will eventually need the expertise of someone else, so why not partner with the best and most brilliant professionals you can find?

Designing a Solid Business Plan

Before investing in anything, you need a solid plan to go with it. The goals that you will create should match with the rental properties that you will be investing in. There are different types of properties that you could invest in. These properties will have an impact on how you will realize your financial goals.

What is your mission statement? The mission statement in your business plan will define the direction that your business will be taking. For instance, your mission could be to provide affordable housing by investing in real estate properties. From this, your mission statement should guide you in settling for affordable houses that will entice your tenants. This is the main goal that you will consider before making any investment decision.

A good plan will also detail the guiding principles that you and your business associates will stick to. Some of the things that you should not forget to include here are the principles that will drive your business to succeed.

Your plan should also detail the way in which service should be provided to tenants. This gives your team members a reason to understand that without the tenants that business would not have been present. Your business plan should also include the market analysis that you will have to focus on before investing in any rental property. Here, you will have to consider factors such as the industry analysis at large, the specific market size, industry participants, competitors and the market segments. Having the right information about the market will help you make sound decisions about the best property investments that you should choose.

Chapter 3: Property Wholesaling

If you are starting your real estate career as a wholesaler, then you should be familiar with how wholesalers operate, as that will make it easier for you to connect with other wholesalers.

But regardless of whether you are starting your career with this method or not, it is important to note that wholesalers can serve as one great source of finding great deals. Usually, they will mark up the properties so that they can profit from them, but that is perfectly okay - after all, profit is what drives business. However, if you must use wholesalers, ensure you make them understand clearly that you will only want them sending you deals that are off-market, not deals that anyone can find on the internet.

Real estate industry events and local real estate clubs are good places to find wholesalers. Spread your card around and let them know you are interested in being added to their list of buyers.

If you live in a state that does require you to get your real estate license in order to officially wholesale properties, you can either proceed down that route which will have multiple ancillary benefits for your real estate investment career, or if you are anxious to get started, you can instead perform essentially the same process via what is known as a double close. In this instance you would arrange to purchase a property and then sell your new property so that the two transactions overlap as much as possible while still allowing the purchase of the property to go through before the sale does. This type of transaction is not always possible depending on the type of contact you sign with the original seller.

Become a licensed real estate agent

If you plan on frequently wholesaling properties, then you might find it more useful to instead simply break down and get your real estate license. In most cases this process will only take a few months and the savings offered can be substantial, even after actual costs and time costs have been factored in. As with the wholesale process in general, every state is different when it comes to exactly what is required to get your real estate license, though the basics tend to be at least 18 years old, US citizen and a successful completion of a real estate education course.

Education courses are also going to vary and can be taught by licensed education facilities, real estate offices, online or at state or community colleges. They tend to be between 40 and 60 hours and often cost several hundred dollars. Even after the education course has been completed it is important to also schedule time to take a licensing preparation course as it will often include information not covered in the education course.

With all the studying behind you it is recommended that you then make it a point to take the licensing test as quickly as possible to ensure that everything you learn remains fresh in your mind when you need to put it to use. You will also need to submit to a background check and offer up your fingerprints and often provide additional information as well. It is important to know what you need to have in order to be eligible for the test as acquiring certain materials can take several weeks.

After you have successfully completed the test you are going to need to find a broker that you are interested in working with, even if you only ever plan on facilitating your own sales. Brokers are always on the lookout for new real estate agents which means you will want to look around for the one that will give you the best benefits. You may also need what is known as error and omission insurance depending on your state.

Getting the right property at the right price

As a property wholesaler, you are going to be working with a margin that is even smaller than what the average property flipper is working with because you need to find room to make a profit somewhere between the ARV, the cost of the remodel, the 30 percent flipper profit margin and everything else that goes into getting a property truly ready to sell. With all this in mind, you are going to want to try and make a minimum of $5,000 on every sale to ensure it is worth your while. Even when using your most creative property finding techniques, you are likely to naturally come across properties that you can wholesale far less often than properties that can be flipped as normal. What this means in practice is that if you want to find the right types of properties to wholesale for a profit, you are going to have to negotiate for them. Remember, the amount you can make on a given wholesale is going to depend entirely on you, keep the following tips in mind to ensure things always end up in your favor.

Approach the right way

While negotiating contracts and service agreements so that they work out to your advantage is a useful and potentially valuable skill, many people shy away from it because they approach the act with the feeling that they are doing something untoward. In reality, however, there is nothing in the rules of negotiation that says that both parties cannot walk away satisfied which means that negotiations only end negatively if you let them move in that direction.

Establish trust early

Any good negotiation is going to be built on the trust that the other party is going to act in good faith. As you typically won't have much time to generate the type of rapport that trust requires, it is important that you work quickly if you want the negotiation to proceed as smoothly as possible. To start you are going to always want to prioritize making a good first impression before striving to find common hobbies and interests. Try and bring in a bit of humor to the proceedings and if that fails then flattery should be used as a last resort as it can easily be perceived as gauche.

Determine the relative power levels

When it comes to negotiating effectively, in order to do so you are going to need to get an accurate read on the overall level of power that you have in relation to the other party. To do this you are going to want to determine the other viable alternatives the other party has outside of the terms you have suggested. The more viable options that the other party has, the less strength you have in the negotiations and the more carefully you will need to tread if you hope for things to work to your advantage.

Listen

A good negotiator listens as much as they speak, both to what the other party is saying as well as to what they are avoiding bringing up in conversation. With practice, you will be surprised at just how much you can learn from the other negotiator simply by truly listening to what they have to say. While being an important part of any negotiation on its own, LISTEN is also a useful way to remember several other key behaviors you should be mindful of using during every negotiation.

Wholesaling contracts

Once you have successfully negotiated a great price on a property and have the contract in hand, the last thing that you need to do is to find a seller that you can count on to take the property off your hand. Luckily, if you have already started working with a real estate investment club then this part is often quite easy. All you need to do is to find a property flipper who is known to work in cash or has access to a reliable stream of private money loans. As the right property for wholesaling isn't likely to come around every day, it is likely that you will only need to find a single buyer who will be willing to snatch up anything you bring them.

Four Strategies for Finding Buyers

Call advertisements/signs put by different investors

You have seen those signs that state "we purchase houses" or promotions in the paper that state something comparative. These are investors that have put a development since they need somebody to present to them an arrangement. You should call these individuals and inquire as to whether you found a method that seemed well and good, would they be intrigued. You would then be able to discover what they are searching for in an agreement. At that point, you will comprehend what they are searching for, and you are beginning to fabricate a rundown of buyers.

Join real estate investing affiliations

Real estate financial specialist affiliations are gatherings of nearby investors that need a spot to arrange. Since you are searching for investors to buy your agreements, here is an excellent spot to go to discover them. Use Google to seek with your city and "real estate investing relationship" to perceive what you have locally. This is an extraordinary asset for discovering buyers for your agreements.

Spot an advertisement and get buyers calling you

With the extraordinary arrangement that you have, you can put a promotion in the paper or on the Internet and have buyers call you. Incredible arrangements will always draw in intrigued buyers. You can complete a touch of advertising and get individuals calling you.

Utilize person to person communication

Technology has now made the structure a rundown of buyers simpler than it ever has been. Spots like Facebook have bunches that you can join explicitly for wholesaling. There are wholesaling gatherings, money, purchaser gatherings, etc. When you have joined these gatherings, you have moment access to an extensive system of buyers.

If you have not investigated this asset, you ought to invest some energy joining these gatherings. It can take your investing to an unheard-of level.

Chapter 4: Investing in Rental Properties

What are the first steps that are you need to take before you make a Rental Properties deal? Evaluate your personal finances. Nothing can happen, nothing can be purchased without finances being in place.

Even if you only have enough for a deposit on one property and plant for any repairs or renovation if needed, you need to know how this investment is going to fit into your personal finances.

You need to prepare a personal income statement outlining your finances. Understand what income you have, subtracting all the necessary essentials needed to live, debts and savings all calculated to give you a clear picture as to what finances you have to capitalize in a property, as well as monies set aside for maintenance and repairs. The financial statement will give you a total picture of what you have for your investment capital.

Now comes the decision making - how much should you invest? The answer is within the capital you have, the budget you will be comfortable with and mathematics. Again, even if you have enough for one property investment, it is key to know exactly what you can do when investing, so you don't get into any financial difficulties.

Discipline is a crucial factor in making money with rental properties as you must not think of a second property as an ATM. In fact, whatever profits you make, part of them will have to be reinvested into the property at some point.

In order to ensure this discipline, I recommend having a separate bank account specifically for the property. For example, your tenant may choose to deposit their rent into that account. So, you would only need to withdraw the money needed to cover the mortgage payments and taxes. The rest stays in that account. Over time, it will add up.

One other very important expense to consider is that when tenants move out, you may not rent the property out immediately. In fact, it may sit there for a month or two. In the meantime, you need to cover the mortgage and utility payments. This is money that you will get back when you rent the property out again, but it is a common pitfall with rental properties.

In addition, you might have tenants who fall behind on their rent. But, you are on the hook for making the mortgage payments. So, this is where having that extra cushion can keep you from paying these expenses out of your own pocket.

Naturally, no investment is devoid of risk. There is always a risk attached to all investments. There are no exceptions. These reflections are intended to help you manage risk and be aware of what you are getting yourself into. Consequently, your ability to foresee these risks will enable you to keep your head above water and generate profits from your rental property.

So then, what is the point of investing in rental properties if I may not be able to actually make money off of it?

An erroneous view on investments is that successful investments produce cash. Some folks get it completely wrong by thinking that rental properties will allow them to quit their jobs and enable them to live off that income. And yes, that is possible if you have enough properties producing enough cash per month in order to sustain your lifestyle.

The reality though is that investments serve two purposes: one is to make your initial investment grow over time and eventually leave you with more money than you put it. The other purpose is to protect your money's purchasing power over time.

This second point is very important, and it is the reason why you can't just leave your money under the mattress. In the modern economy, inflation will slowly eat away at your money.

When you put your money into real estate, you can hedge your investment by raising rents every time you get a new tenant. Of course, you can't hike up the rent too high because you need to take the market into consideration. If rents become stagnant, then you can't hike up the rent too much because renters simply won't pay it. But if the market is hot, then you can hike up your rent in tandem with the market.

Also, you will commonly see and hear how investing in real estate is a great way for you to save up for retirement. Again, you would ideally have paid off any and all mortgages by the time you retire. That means that the cash you get from your rents will go straight into your pocket. This, combined with other savings and investments, will allow you to retire within your means. But younger folks should be keen on keeping their jobs and sustaining that income.

With rental properties, your focus should be to stay in compliance with building codes and maintaining a decent property for your renters.

Risks Involved in Owning a Rental Property

Firstly, there is always the risk that tenants will damage the property. This is quite common and can jack up maintenance costs when tenants move out. This type of damage goes beyond the usual fresh coat of paint or new carpet that needs to be put in. In some cases, larger repairs need to be made. For example, broken fixtures, tiles, and even flooring can become costly. Also, there are cases where children can punch holes in drywall and pets can cause serious damage.

If a property has been seriously damaged, the repairs can be deducted from the renter's security deposit. However, it's not that simple. The damage needs to be properly documented and estimates need to be drawn up by contractors in order to justify the deduction. This could pose a complicated situation especially if the tenant chooses to fight it.

Insurance on rental properties does set limits on how much damage you can claim on it, but it can keep you from having to cover unexpected repairs out of pocket. However, this is an additional expense attached to the property. But have no fear, you can claim it as a deduction.

Another serious risk is having a renter default on their payments. While this would trash the renter's credit, a bankruptcy court can clear the obligation on the part of the renter. That leaves the owner with no means of getting that money back. Once again, insurance can cover lost rent up to a certain maximum. This varies according to the insurer and it certainly pays to shop around.

If you choose to go the way of short-term rentals, collecting fees upfront is the best way to protect yourself from not getting paid. In a sense, it works just like a hotel. Platforms such as Airbnb have protection built in to ensure that even if someone flakes on a booking, the owner is still compensated for that loss.

There is one other very important reason for insurance on rental properties: accidents. There is always the possibility that an accident could occur on the property. For instance, someone trips down the stairs and decides to sue the landlord for negligence. Insurance would keep you from bearing the brunt of the lawsuit. Even if the landlord is held liable, insurance can kick in and protect you from being wiped out. You may think that's a bit extreme, but it happens.

As for the major risks involved in owning rental property, the biggest risk is associated with financials. For example, being unable to cover the mortgage payments, particularly if the property sits empty. This may seem extreme, but given certain situations, it can.

Chapter 5: Investing in Real Estate via IRA

If you are interested in investing in real estate with the help of an IRA (individual retirement account) then there are plenty of unique pitfalls that you will need to be aware of if you hope to do so successfully, though there are also plenty of benefits that make it worth the effort when handled correctly. An IRA is a type of long term investment account that was created in the early 1970s as a way for financially responsible individuals without company sponsored retirement plans to prepare for their future and to reward them for doing so. As such, IRAs allow individuals to defer access to profits from numerous different types of investments in exchange for having access to a greater overall portion of those funds when they reach retirement age, or earlier if they are willing to pay an early withdrawal fee for doing so.

While, technically, a real estate IRA is no different than an average IRA, in practice it is unique because it means the IRA can be used to purchase something outside the realm of what most IRAs deal in. What's more, most IRAs will not allow for this type of investment which means you will need to be a part of an IRA that is self-directed to use your

IRA as a real estate investment tool. They type of real estate that you are going to invest in isn't limited either and it can be in any of the common types including residential real estate, raw land, commercial real estate or anything else you are interested in.

Hard and fast real estate IRA rules

While there are numerous benefits to IRA real estate investment if you are looking for a long term real estate investment, there are several rules that you are going to want to keep in mind so you know just what it is you are getting into. First and foremost, it is important to keep in mind that the real estate IRA that you create cannot legally purchase any property that you own.

Furthermore, you cannot purchase property from anyone who is considered a disqualified person which is any business you are a part or whole owner of as well as any property that is owned by your current or previous spouse, your parents or any grandparents or variation thereon, your children, anyone married or previously married to your children, grandchildren **etc.** Furthermore, you cannot purchase property from IRA service providers or companies that an IRA service provider holds a major share in.

Additionally, you are not allowed to profit from the IRA ownership of a property which means you can't use your real estate IRA to buy the vacation house you rent every year or the office building that happens to house the office that you rent as well. The sole purpose of an IRA is to provide you with a benefit at a predetermined point in the future and it breaks the rules set forth if you or anyone set forth as a disqualified person benefits from what the IRA is doing at a point prior to this.

Not only can you expressly not take advantage of the property while the IRA owns it, you are not even allowed to do work or renovations on the property yourself without worrying about paying a series of ever increasing fees for the privilege. As such, when you are looking for property to direct your real estate IRA to purchase, it is important you do so with a clear idea of what the relevant renovation costs are going to be before you move forward as there is no way for you to work off the difference if you misestimate just what all needs to be done.

Furthermore, it is important to keep in mind that any property that your IRA purchases is going to need to be officially owned by the IRA which is a separate entity compared to you as an individual. Additionally, you will want to keep in mind that property your purchase using your IRA doesn't need to be funded exclusively through the IRA, investments can use only part of an IRA fund, you just need to speak with a financial advisor so you ensure that everything is structured properly to prevent yourself from accidentally breaking the rules. If you do choose to use a traditional method of financing for your IRA real estate investment, then you will want to be aware of the fact that you will have to pay taxes on the property as per the rules for unrelated business income taxes.

Remember, when a property is owned by your IRA it is important that any costs related to the property be deducted from the IRA account and only from the IRA account. This includes things like home owner association fees, general bills, property taxes, improvement costs and anything else that is required for the IRA owned property. Along these same lines then, it is important that all profits that come from the property in question are also exclusively the domain of the IRA as well. You will be able to access the profits eventually, it will typically just take a while. In general, you are eligible to start using the profits generated from an IRA once you reach the age of 59.5, though this is not always the case and different IRAs have different requirements.

While there are plenty of tax related benefits to using a real estate IRA, it is important to keep in mind what tax benefits you are giving up as well. Specifically, if the IRA owns the property then this means that you will not get to take a deduction on the property based on depreciation. You can also not claim any other deductions or losses related to the property. Finally, it is important to keep in mind that you are legally required to cash in on your IRA by the time you are 71 years old which means that if the property is still in the IRAs name at this point and cannot be easily sold you can be in for some potential issues.

Chapter 6: Property management

Maintaining rental properties is very similar to maintaining your own home. You keep it clean, fix things when they break, and replace items when they get old. The overall look of a rental unit is what appeals to tenants. If the rental is clean, maintained, and in good condition, the owner can rent it at a higher price.

Repairs and Maintenance

When you get that call from a tenant that something either broke, needs a general repair, or is scheduled for maintenance, make sure you and the tenant communicate about the work that needs to be done by using a **Tenant Maintenance & Repair Request.** If this request process is not stated in your rental agreements, you can always add it by adding an addendum and sending the tenant a copy. The addendum should state that you are adding a new policy that now requires all tenants to fill out a **Tenant Maintenance & Repair Request** if they wish any repairs or maintenance to be done. Also, add to the addendum that in case of an emergency the tenants are required to call you immediately, but still send in the request form to schedule repair of the damage.

Inspections

Typically, inspections on your property are done monthly, quarterly, or annually depending on what needs to be inspected and what kind of condition your property is in. You may want to drive by your rental once a month to see how it looks visually from the outside. If the yard looks neglected, it's a safe bet the tenants are probably not keeping up the inside as well. For example, you may want to have quarterly inspections if you notice your tenant has lots of trash that is not in or near the trash cans. At the very least, I would suggest doing an annual inspection of the inside and outside of your rental to check things like steps and walkways, smoke detectors, carbon monoxide detectors, pipes, and overall appearance of the unit. Send the tenants a **Twenty-Four-Hour Notice of Intent to Enter** form and do a quick, yet thorough, inspection.

As a landlord or property manager, you are responsible for keeping the property in habitable condition. The term 'habitable' means that the property must meet safety and health standards as determined by the laws in your local area. If property damage occurs and it is not the result of abuse or neglect by the tenant, and that damage affects the habitability of the property, you are responsible for correcting it. Of course, the tenant also has a responsibility to let you know about the damage.

Recordkeeping & Bookkeeping

Recordkeeping and bookkeeping are so important. This task, if not done at least monthly, can cause an array of problems, such as lost income, unexplained expenses, missing or misplaced documents, the list goes on. Accurate and consistent recordkeeping and bookkeeping are the backbone of a successful business.

There are many types of software programs like Quicken and QuickBooks that property management companies use to do their bookkeeping. If you manage your properties yourself, and don't want to use a computer software program, a simple spreadsheet will do the trick.

Mixing business with personal money makes it difficult to separate your personal income and expenses with your business income and expenses. Thus, making tax preparation much more challenging and opening the door to overlooking deductible receipts.

Tenant Move-In Information

When a tenant moves in they will need to know things like who the electric company is so they can set up service in their name. You will want to have a form for each property, which you give your tenant that includes the contact information for the electric, gas, water, sewer, garbage, telephone, and cable TV companies. You may also wish to provide tenants with other helpful but optional resources such as the contact information for your house cleaner, carpet cleaner, or insurance agent.

Property Maintenance

Having a property is one thing, but sustaining and keeping it relevant is another. Just like our skin, continuous nourishing, care, and regard is what keeps any real estate property glowing (successful). There are steps to sustaining your property, but the first step is having the knowledge on how to sustain it. Knowledge is power, so in order to be relevant in business, you must continuously upgrade your understanding of the real estate market. Remember a clean property that is well taken care of will always call for better clients and at a higher cost.

Unlike your personal household, you won't see your rental properties every day. So you need to become more systematic about inspecting for damage and maintenance issues. You will probably have some tenants who have owned houses, and you will learn over time that you can count on them to alert you to any possible issues. But generally you will want to find excuses to visit occasionally so you can take a look around and see whether anything needs attention.

Dealing with Troublesome Tenants

While most property investors will tell you that the majority of their tenants are a pleasure to work with, you might still end up with a tenant that can turn into a nightmare. As a landlord, you have a good chance that you will run into some type of issue with a tenant. If not handled properly and quickly, having a troublesome tenant renting your property could devastate your investment that you have worked so hard on to achieve. Below are 5 steps in dealing with troublesome tenants.

Build a Positive Relationship

The very first thing you can do to help keep yourself from having issues with your tenant in the first place is by keeping a positive relationship with them. By having a positive relationship, your tenants will more likely treat you and your terms in the same respect. Even when problems arise, treat your tenant in the most professional manner possible. The more professional you treat your tenants, the more likely they will feel ashamed of breaking the terms of your contract or disrespect your investment property.

Deal any Issues Right Away

Nobody likes to deal with conflict. This is especially true when it comes to troublesome tenants. However, the longer you let the issue go unresolved, the harder it becomes to get them fixed. Therefore, it is important to deal with any issues as soon as they arise. If your tenant doesn't make their rent payment on time, jump on the matter as soon as you can. If you are getting disturbance complaints from the neighbors, make sure you notify the tenant and get the issue resolved with the neighbors right away. Procrastinating on any matter with your tenants cannot be an option. The longer you wait with dealing with any tenant issues, the greater you increase your chances of losing revenue from your investment property.

Make the Matter Urgent

When any issue arises, you would want to make the matter extremely urgent. If you handle the issue with a sense of urgency, more than likely will the tenant take your request seriously. One way you can employ to ensure that issues are dealt with urgency includes providing the tenant a written notice for every issue.

Track Everything

Make sure that you document every incident and every step you take towards resolving any issues with your tenants. This is to ensure that you are able to validate all steps you took into getting the issue resolved in case legal action is taken against the tenant or against you. Document every time you attempted to contact the tenant, whenever you mailed any notices out, etc. The more detailed you are, the better you can defend any potential legal case.

Evict the Tenant When Necessary

Evicting a tenant can be extremely difficult. In most circumstances, this requires you to get a court order. There are many reasons that you can evict a tenant. Some of these reasons include not paying the rent, damaging your property, disturbing the peace, or even other reasons that are set in the contract (such as having pets not allowed on the premises). While you can "encourage" the tenants to vacate the premises, you are not generally allowed to kick them off the property yourself. Unfortunately, some tenants are knowledgeable about these restrictions and will use them to their advantage.

If evicting a tenant is required, you must make sure you are following the Landlord and Tenant Act. It is important that you follow every procedure explained within the act or you may end up losing your case if legal action is taken. You can learn more about the Tenant and Landlord act in the References section of this book.

Choosing the Best Property Management Company

Your property management company represents you. In the perception of the tenants, there is no difference between contacting you or someone you hired for maintenance and repairs. They expect to be provided with quality customer service and to have their requests fulfilled in a timely manner. This means that the property management company you hired represents you and your investment properties. Therefore, it is essential that you not only find an affordable company, but also one that will provide the best services to you and your tenants.

Managing The Cash Flow

The income from the real estate business has aided some of the most opulent people in the world in amassing wealth. Even though the majority started as proprietors of smaller multi-unit buildings, they soon expanded to dealing in bigger commercial properties. It is arguable to say that in real estate, earning passive income is the only thing that investors strive for.

In the real estate industry, there are endless means of generating capital; therefore, an investor must appreciate the benefits of understanding the cash flow of the industry in order to seize arising opportunities for the most gain. Of these endless means, a very typical example is rental properties.

Cash flow is the number of earnings an investor has after having paid their total bill; it's how much the investor will most likely take home in the end. This money embodies gains later used for reinvestment in other events or saving for retirement. Succinctly put, cash flow exemplifies an equitable amount of surplus money after accounting for every capital expense made by the investor.

More often than not, investors use estimates from cash flow summations to ascertain the benefits of investing in a particular property. If you are contemplating venturing into rental properties, understanding how cash flow is actuated and knowing the expenses to account for should be a priority.

Chapter 7: Lease options

Lease Options Work as its name implies, the lease option simultaneously creates two contracts: (1) a rental agreement and (2) an option to purchase agreement.

The option contract grants tenant the right to buy the property at some future date. At a minimum, the option will include (1) the up-front fee to the seller as payment for granting the option, (2) the option purchase price for the property, (3) the date on which the purchase option expires, (4) right of assignment, and (5) the amount of any rent credits that will count toward the purchase price of the optioned property.

When it comes to ensuring that you and your future tenant are going to be on the same page, it is important to outline a lease that covers every possible eventuality. The sad fact of the matter is that if you don't specifically outline what can and can't be done on the property, even if it seems impossible to conceive of a world where another person would be willing to do the thing you are imagining, then some tenant is eventually going to go ahead and try it. As such, a well written lease is a good way to cut off miscreant behavior at the bud by making it clear just what it is that you expect from all of your tenants.

You are going to want to clearly outline what you expect when it comes to regular maintenance of the property as well as what constitutes regular trash removal and fair use for the property in general. In addition to outline what is and is not permitted, it is important to clearly outline what the penalty for going against the rules of the lease so that any potential tenants start off their relationship with a clear idea of exactly what is being expected of them. This doesn't mean you are going to want to be draconian in your lease, however, as you will often find that the benefits of being a nice landlord often outweigh the costs. Be fair but firm and you will likely be able to find a balance that you and your tenants can gladly live with.

The Lease Option Sandwich

The lease option sandwich magnifies your potential profit. I nstead of buying a property, you find sellers who will lease-option their property to you at both a bargain rental rate and a bargain price. Typically, these sellers were not advertising their property as a lease option. In fact, they may not even have thought of the idea until you put a proposal in front of them. Through this lease option, you control the property for two to five years. Your cash out of pocket totals less than you would probably have paid in closing costs had you immediately bought the property. Next, you spend some money on spruce-up expenses (if desirable) and Re-advertise the property specifically as a lease option. You find tenant-buyers and sign them up on a lease option with you as the lessor. Your tenant-buyers agree to pay you a higher monthly rent and a higher option price than you've negotiated for yourself in your role as lessee/optionee with the property owners. You profit from the difference. Your rate of return skyrockets because you gain control of a property with almost no cash investment. The up-front money you've collected from your tenant- buyers exceeds the amount you paid to the property owners. Essentially, you buy wholesale and sell retail without investing much cash in inventory.

How to Find Lease Option Buyers and Sellers?

To discover the best deal on a lease option, first talk with sellers who advertise lease options. But these sellers typically retail their properties. You might find it tougher to negotiate a bargain here. Contact motivated for-sale-by-owner (FSBO) sellers in the "Homes for Sale" ads. Or try property owners who are running "House for Rent" ads. As noted, the best lease option sellers may not realize how the idea can benefit them until you suggest it. To learn which type ad or posting pulls the best responses, ask your callers to tell you in which category they saw the ad. Research which listings draw the largest number of qualified callers.

On Lease Terms and Tenants Changing or Breaking the Lease

Your lease protects your interests, those of your tenants, and acts as the cornerstone of your relationship. This is why you must take time to draw up your lease. If you can afford it, go through it thoroughly with your lawyer.

On Tenants Wanting to Change the Lease

At some point, the tenant may want to change the lease. For instance, he or she may need to replace a roommate or perhaps extend the lease term. You must not feel pressured to bow to the tenant's requests. While the first section talks about appealing to the tenant's sentiments, you must remember to appeal to your own as well. Take time to study the changes the tenant has in mind.

You should make it known that for major lease term changes, the tenant needs to make his or her request in writing. This will give you a chance to consider the tenant's request without the pressure of having to respond immediately. A written request will also do a good job of clarifying what the tenant needs changed.

On Tenants Breaking the Lease

This is usually a massive inconvenience to both you and your tenant. In many states, it qualifies as a breach of contract. What this means is that technically, your tenant is obligated to pay the rent for the rest of the lease term even if he or she moves out early. However, as is the case with most contracts in the country, you are obligated to "mitigate damages" as a party to a contract. What this means to you as a landlord is that you must go to work finding a new tenant as fast as you can.

If a tenant needs to break the lease, he/she must bring this to your attention as quickly as possible. Do not feel pressured to be flexible. However, if the tenant helps bring in a new tenant, do not stand in his/her way.

Lease, license and tenancy

It is a contract giving the exclusive right of possession and use of landed property for a fixed or determinable period, usually in consideration of the payment of rent.

Tenancy is the transfer of a right to use/possession giving to a prospective tenant by a property manager on behalf of a landlord or from a landlord to a tenant.

It is a written agreement between the former and the latter lasting for a relatively short period, monthly, weekly or annually in consideration of a payment of rent.

Tenancy is for a short period while lease usually indicates a more enduring interest.

The right given by the license cannot be conveyed to another individual, since a license is not an appurtenant right but is a personal right, and thus does not benefit another property.

As with an easement, the holder of a license does not usually pay rent for the right to use the burdened property.

A license agreement often arises from an informal agreement between a property owner and a neighbor or friend. For example, a property owner may accept an offer by their neighbor to jointly or separately make use of the owner's property. Thus, the neighbor is given a license to use the property and agrees to maintain or improve the property for the agreed privileges.

Chapter 8: Flipping Real Estate

When it comes to getting started at flipping real estate, the first thing you are going to need to learn to do is to accurately determine the ARV (After Repair Value) of the properties that you are looking at. The ARV is the amount you can realistically expect to sell the property for once it is perfect and being able to do so effectively will help ensure you don't get stuck with a lemon that ends up costing you more than it is worth just to get rid of it. You can do research to determine what these amounts are likely to be, but the most reliable way to track down this information is via practice. After you have looked at a hundred or so properties you will likely find that you have gotten much better at pegging current retail value.

Types of Flipping

Wholesaling is when you buy a property and immediately resell it for a profit. You don't do any major repair or maintenance so you don't put up any money for the house. It's important you're a strong negotiator or this won't work. You must convince a seller to sell their property at well-below market value then convince the buyer to pay you near market value money.

Rehabbing is when you buy property that's in disrepair, fix it up, then sell it. You can choose to focus on houses that need some minor repairs or tackle larger projects (e.g. houses with structural problems, fire damage, water damage).

Active versus passive real estate investment opportunities

When it comes to making the decision to invest in real estate via flipping houses, it is important to understand the difference between actively investing in real estate and passive real estate investment income streams. For starters, the buy and hold real estate investment strategy can be thought of as a form of passive real estate investment, especially if you plan on using a real estate management company to take care of all of the day to day landlord duties. What this means is that while you will have to be paying attention to the market and looking for viable properties, a majority of your time is only going to ever be spent waiting for the money to roll in.

Things to keep in mind when starting out

As a new house flipper it is going to likely feel as though the sheer number of things you need to keep in mind when it comes to finding the right properties to be successful is weighing you down and keeping you from moving forward successfully. When this happens you will want to keep in mind the fact that it will definitely get easier with practice as well as the following tips for success.

Sometimes you just need to jump in

While it is always going to behoove you to do as much research on a given property as well as the state of the market as a whole as possible, that doesn't need you need to be a real estate expert in order to actually make your first flip. On the contrary, you don't need to worry about knowing everything, as long as you can come to terms with what it is you know and where your blind spots are. Remember, as long as you know enough to know when you are getting in over your depth you can reach out to individuals more adequately qualified to help you out of the corner you may have found yourself in.

Understand that marketing is just as important as renovating

It doesn't matter how good of a potential deal you are currently sitting on if there is no one around to take advantage of it. Unfortunately, many new real estate flippers find themselves in just this situation as they have focused all of their time and energy on finding and renovating the perfect property without giving enough thought to where the potential buyers are ultimately going to come from. This means you are ultimately going to want to spend as much time thinking how you are going to market the property when it is finished for a reasonable budget as you are deciding how to best find and renovate ideal properties.

Reach out to the local investment community

While you might not initially expect real estate investors to be a social bunch, the reality of the matter is that they have much more to gain from collaborating than they do from fighting with one another at all times, especially if they aren't going after the same types of property. As such, the odds are good that if you live in even a relatively small city you will be able to find a local real estate investment club that can provide you with a wide variety of useful information as long as you take the time to ask. A local real estate investment club is an invaluable resource as its members will be able to clue you in on market specifics that it might take years for you to pick up on for yourself.

You can't win if you don't play

When it comes to finding properties that are worth the effort that will be required to flip them, it is important to keep in mind that you will never be the winning bid on a property that you didn't make an offer on. Many new real estate investors can determine if a property could be successfully flipped and even determine the costs that would make it worth their while and yet they balk when it comes to actually making the offer because they feel a lowball bid is insulting.

Estimating Repairs

Estimating repairs is a skill indeed, but you need not worry too much because it's a fairly a rather easy one to learn. The first step is by determining WHAT needs to be repaired, you're going to have to keep your Comps in mind when you're estimating the repairs and determining WHAT needs to be done. The WHAT is much more important than the HOW at this point. There is no need to get bogged down by details at this stage in the game. It is more important to make sure you have a close ballpark price on what it's going to cost to perform the necessary repairs. The key point here is 'NECESSARY REPAIRS'.

MUST items are of course anything that must be done. Basically, these are items that would stop an average potential buyer for that market from buying or making an offer on your home.

Finding a Flip-Worthy Home

For beginners, there might only be two ways of seeing potential flips - the first is **too risky** and the second is **too easy.** Don't worry - everyone started out looking through the same two-toned glasses. But you can hone your eye for investment to break through the initial impression and see what's **really** there.

Not every house you see will translate to an easy sale, and not all of them will flop. As an investor, you need to understand that there are **intrinsic** factors that add to the salability of a house, and that the future of your investment doesn't solely rely on your capacity to mitigate risks and avoid mistakes.

So what are some of the factors you can use to determine whether or not a potential property will make you the profits you want?

Location, Location, Location

Location is a key factor in salability because it tells your buyers whether this is a place where **they can grow some roots**. Individuals seeking to purchase immovable property with the purpose of **living in it** want to make sure they'd get to enjoy the convenience of living in a place that suits their lifestyle.

Physical Characteristics

The **physical characteristics** of the property will play a major role in profit because that's **all you have to go on** in terms of how far you can flip your property.

Remember, unless you're willing to cut back on your profit just so you can spend more on bigger, more extensive renovations, the smarter choice would be to spend as little on repairs as possible while generating the most positive change. So what your chosen property brings to the table is essentially what it will look like after the renovations are done - with a few improvements of course.

Expenditures and Potential Profit

The good news is that diving into fix and flips can be extremely lucrative. The bad news is that you need to actually do the math in order to find out whether or not there's any profit in a house you've chosen.

While there's a completely separate, in-depth discussion on computations later on, it's important to get this information out of the way at this point just to give you a fuller understanding of the **factors** that make up a good purchase. For now, we'll focus on the basic **financial terms** that you need to wrap your head around so that the rest of this guide makes sense.

Arrange to Complete Big Repairs Early

If part of your renovation scheme involves highly intrusive procedures such as knocking down walls or replacing an entire floor, then you should seek to do these procedures sooner rather than later, ideally before you and your family move into the house. For example, if you decide that you want to knock down a wall, do it early and give all the dust time to settle. When you do begin moving your stuff in, try to separate your primary living areas and your possessions from the major construction sites within the home.

Ways to Keep Renovation Costs Low

Efficiency of Space

While it may be glamorous to add square footage to the kitchen by building a large addition, sometimes a perceived lack of space can be remedied by diversifying the space that's given. Rather than build up/out, build within by maximizing usable surface areas. Instead of expanding the kitchen out into the yard, sometimes replacing half of a wall for a breakfast bar is all you need. Maximizing the amount of horizontal planes wherever you can will eliminate the need for more square footage. Upgraded cabinetry can be expensive, sure, but it will cost you a fraction of what you could have spent on a large addition.

Limit the Amount of Lighting Fixtures

You want to cut down on installing recessed lighting whenever possible. The fixtures themselves can be costly enough, but there's also a lot of labor in cutting out individual holes and insulating them. A single overhead fixture can even produce more wattage than a handful of recessed light bulbs, and cost you several hundred dollars less. Maximizing the effect of natural light can also go a long way. You'd be surprised how much proper drapery can let in ample light.

Use Recycled Materials

You can drastically cut down your renovation costs by using recycled or lightly used building materials. One terrific resource is a Habitat for Humanity ReStore. These places provide repurposed materials and fixtures for roughly 50% of what you would pay at a Home Depot or Lowe's. You would be surprised at how much can be collected from these stores. Prehung doors, skylights and windows, insulation, and flooring are just a few things that can be found here.

You can also inquire if your subcontractors have any materials left over from previous jobs that can be repurposed for your project. Especially with things like flooring, sheetrock, and lumber, it's certainly worth investigating.

Don't Move the Sink or Toilet

Though it may seem like an odd addition to this list, it costs a lot more than you may think to relocate plumbing fixtures. Rerouting pipes and tinkering with water flow can easily become the largest part of your plumbing rehab price. Try to leave the sinks and toilets where they are when conceiving your new plan.

Develop a Plan Early and Stick to It

You want to have as fully thought-out a plan as possible before you start doing any of the demolition. Know what types of fixtures and appliances you want, and how much they will cost beforehand. You can never be too specific. A common mistake is to rely on the subcontractor's allowance without making sure the two of you are in total agreement on what is to be put in. Allowances are almost always too low, and you don't want to get slapped with a higher estimate when the subcontractor thought you wanted a slightly different material installed.

Minimizing your renovation cost is a very nuanced process, and will likely take some trial-and-error in developing a sound system. The suggestions outlined above are but a starting outline for ways you can look to save. The important thing to remember is that no amount of savings is too minute; it all adds up to sizable dollars in the end.

Putting Your Property on the Market

At this point it can be easy for new real estate investors to overprice their properties in hopes that they can make as much as possible on their first flip. Unfortunately, the only thing that overpricing your property is going to do is to make your property sit on the market for much longer than it otherwise would. Remember, your goal is to have as many successfully flipped properties as possible and pricing your property competitively is a big part of ensuring things keep moving along smoothly.

Private Selling

Aside from posting online however, private selling also entails direct mail that you'd have to execute by yourself. Putting up posters, handing out flyers around your property should help draw attention - but it can eat up quite a lot of your time.

Real Estate Agents

Hiring a realtor might be your best bet if you feel like you'd want to be a little less hands-on when finding a possible buyer. These experts can list your home in a variety of exclusive websites (like the MLS) and draw more attention towards your listing because well, that's what they do best!

Auctions

Just as you might have visited a few auctions to discover possible houses for your venture, so too can you sell your investment through an auction. The beauty of auction sales is that you get your cash upfront, as soon as that gavel strikes the podium.

Chapter 9: Investing in Vacation Rentals

These can be very lucrative, although you will need to bear in mind that the season is only as long as the weather permits it to be. You need to thus establish whether you will get all the year round letting or whether this will be confined to a set number of weeks. You will also need to find out what the current booking situation is as this will give you a good idea about how reliable your information is and how much work you will need to do to maximize the potential rental. As stated previously, if you live in an area that has a set high season, are you likely to make enough money from the rental income during that high season to be able to pay your debt on a monthly basis – even off season?

There are advantages and disadvantages to considering this kind of rental property. Tourists and people on vacation generally need more attention than tenants would on a regular basis. For example, you may have to deal with regular cleaning and servicing of the rented property in between lets, but there is much more to this than meets the eye. You will also need to ensure that your property is kept up to scratch all the way through the season as people who rent this kind of accommodation expect to get their money's worth. The time that this can work is when you buy into an existing business and sometimes this comes up when the current owner is retiring. Getting your accountant to look at the books will help you to establish the kind of money the previous owner made on the property, bearing in mind the public liability insurance that you would need to ensure is in place for the whole time that the properties are let.

You have a bigger responsibility when you are letting vacation homes because these letting units have to meet the expectations of the tenants and there will be a lot more attention to detail needed to keep your visitors satisfied.

Buying into vacation rentals in other countries may just be the answer. These may be cheaper than properties in your area and there are some great deals to be made where you are given a standard charge to do all the legwork, such as cleaning between lets, maintenance of common areas and let's face it, countries abroad may just appeal to holidaymakers and offer a longer season, thus making it very viable indeed that you can end up with a vacation let that actually pays for itself.

Before you decide to go on this route, you need to make sure of the rules that apply in the country chosen because there are restrictive clauses in many purchases that disallow foreign investment. However, this is only in a few locations in the world, so it is worth talking to your lawyer about it and checking out the viability. For example, you may find that you can afford several apartments in a ski resort or even on a complex that has staff available to do the day to day running of the vacation home.

It is quite possible that you may find somewhere in your own country, though if you do, you need to be sure that you will actually be able to rent the properties on a regular basis in order to meet your loan payments. That's the hard part with vacation rentals although if you have bought into several apartments in the same block, you can double your income over the summer period to cover for the months when the apartment will be empty. Only enter into this kind of deal if you have done your math, or you may end up not having enough to meet your commitments and if you care about your credit score, then you certainly need to have professional advice as to the viability of your plans.

In places where it is warm all the year around, you don't have the same pressure because people will be looking for warm places to escape to in the winter and this means that the potential of letting exists all the year round. That's a good thing because you will be able to pay your debts and gain some extra revenue from the places that you buy. Another benefit with this is that you can actually use the premises for your own vacations, thus using excess rent from your visitors to finance your own vacations! That's got to be a bonus. When you do stay in one of your vacation rentals it also gives you a good idea of how you can improve the service that you are offering clients, so that you can justify increased rent for the future. Vacation rentals are not for the weak-hearted. You will need to be on top of your game as a poor season may leave your struggling to keep up your payments. If you doubt your ability to make money, stick to more traditional rentals because you will get a steady flow of income and will not experience the same dilemma. Yes, traditional rentals earn less but sometimes having that guaranteed monthly income is a better option because it is a more secure option with a rental amount depending upon the units being rented out on a set time based lease that puts you in better control of your income projections. Vacation rentals, on the other hand, can be more lucrative if you are able to organize these well in advance and have all the necessary advertising in place to lure potential clients.

Chapter 10: Investing in Turnkey Property

A turnkey property is any property that can be purchased with the promise of generating cash flow as quickly as possible, in some cases already with renters attached. There are two primary ways of going about finding a turnkey property to purchase, the first provides greater returns, and the second provides the simplest buying experience possible. First of all, if you are interested in making as much off of a property as possible, your best bet is to find a property that is ready rent out immediately, do the leg work of finding a tenant and then find a property management company who will take you on as a client. Once you have put all of the pieces together yourself, you will find that you manage to retain about 90 percent of the total rental price each month.

This is another way to turn your real estate business into a passive one, and I would recommend this for persons who may not really have the time to focus on the hassles of running a real estate business. You can simply choose a turnkey rental company that will do all the work for you - finding the property, fixing it, and renting it out. Some turnkey rental companies also handle property management. So, if you are in a different city, for example, you can use a turnkey real estate company to own an investment property and earn passive income from it.

It doesn't matter if you are a beginner or an experienced real estate investor; this strategy is suitable for anyone who can afford the services of a turnkey rental company. But if you choose to use a turnkey rental company, keep the following in mind:

- Be sure to get an independent inspector and appraiser for the property inspection, rental rate verification, etc. Do not depend on the company's inspector.

- Be wary of turnkey rental companies that want to use the scarcity language to sweet-talk you into buying immediately. There are some of these companies that use dishonest tactics like showing you a rental property, and then when you call back in a couple of hours or the very next day, they tell you it's sold. That way, when they show you another "great" property, you may jump at the opportunity without due consideration so that someone else will not buy it.

Alternatively, you can go through a turnkey property company that specializes in working with investors just like you. In this case you would only need to choose the company you are interested in working with, pay them for a property and then wait for the profits to roll in. In most instances you can expect to both pay more for the property up front and also see a smaller return from each month's rent when going this route. On the other hand, in most cases when you purchase a turnkey property from a turnkey company you can expect to start making money back on your investment the very next month.

As you will be planning to hire a professional management company anyway, it is important to understand that the biggest difference between the two is typically going to be how involved you want to be in the process of investment property ownership. While a property management company means you won't have to deal with the property on the regular, issues may arise from time to time that will still require your attention. On the other hand, turkey company property means you will never have to think of the property outside of when you see profits from your investment show up in your bank account.

Turnkey properties are a perfectly valid choice for any real estate investor, regardless of their location, but it is especially useful for those who like the idea of investing in real estate but find themselves living in an area known for its high costs. In these instances, investors can utilize a turnkey property company to ensure their property is well taken care of, even if it is halfway across the country. Additionally, this type of acquisition can allow anyone anywhere to take advantage of the low property prices that some areas possess.

Understand the risks

One of the biggest misconceptions that many individuals have about investing in real estate via turnkey properties is that every property that is labeled turnkey is automatically going to be a sound real estate investment. Just because a property doesn't require renovation, however, is no reason to assume that it is automatically worth the asking price. As such, you are going to want to apply just as much due diligence to any property that you are purchasing under the turnkey banner as you would any other investment that you make.

If you are making a go of it yourself, this means you are going to want to get to know a local property inspector who you can call when it comes time to find a new investment property. If you are using a turnkey company you are still going to want to go and physically see the property in question, if you don't and the investment fails at a later date, you will only have yourself to blame.

Additionally, you are going to want to go above and beyond when it comes to researching the property management company or turnkey property company that you choose to work with. More so than with many other types of real estate investment, the team that you choose to work with is going to have a major impact on the overall success or failure of your investment which means that you are going to be mindful of this fact when it comes to finding the right one for you, especially if you are several states away from actual location of the property in question. This means you are going to want to have a clear idea of the overall level of experience they have, the costs and the ways that results are reported, at the bare minimum so that you know what to expect.

Overall, it is important to understand that like any other type of investing, investing in real estate via turnkey rental properties is never going to be completely free of risk, no matter what the current state of the market might be. On the other hand, with a few notable exceptions, real estate is always going to be considered a reliable investment that is not prone to many of the fluctuation issues that plague many other types of investment. As with any investment, if you want to know if investing in turnkey real estate is right for you, all you need to do is consider the potential profit and then determine if that justifies the related risk in your eyes and then act accordingly.

Chapter 11: Investing in Commercial Real Estate (Apartment building, offices and warehouses, Retail centers, Hotels and Resorts, Land development)

This section is going to look at whether the time is ripe for commercial real estate investment. It shall also delve into the questions you should ask yourself before you decide to "get in," as well as the decisions you need to make to ensure you survive longer than most.

Ask Yourself These Questions First

Your answers to the following questions shall help you gain immense clarity of thought and action. Answer these questions as honestly and candidly as you can. Preferably, jot the answers in a notebook so that you give yourself to expound and personalize the answer as you deem fit:

Do I have the necessary funds to invest in commercial property?

You may already know; nonetheless, we shall include it here for effect: commercial properties are always substantially more expensive than the likes of residential properties. As such, it is important to ensure that you have sufficient investment capital. If money is somewhat thin, this book will show you different strategies you can follow to fund your investment.

Do I have any financial, trade, or business expertise that may prove valuable to my investment in commercial property?

This one is not a must-have. However, if you have some form of expertise that could be valuable to your investment strategy, such knowledge or expertise shall come in handy since it could steer you down a natural investment path. This will mean that right off the bat, you will have found a niche that works great for you, which will maximize your efficiency as well as the probability to succeed.

Important Decisions to Make Regarding Your Commercial Property Investing

As you let the answers to the questions above marinate, consider the following decisions that you need to make

Decision 1: Decide how you want to invest in commercial property goes

What is it that you want to be? What roles do you want to play? Are you interested in being a landlord who is in ownership of commercial property or does it suit you better to be part of an investment group that purchases office buildings co-operatively?

When you work on your own, you will be shouldering all the risks and responsibilities that come with the package. However, as opposed to being part of an investment group, you will also be taking the whole cake home. Decide what you want to do with your investment ventures.

Decision 2: Decide how much money you can invest as well as how you will finance your investment

When it comes to funding your foray into commercial real estate investing, you can take several financing routes such as traditional loans, partnership investing, hard money loans, crowdfunding and so forth.

The Objectives to Work Toward Investing in Commercial Property

As far as investing in commercial property goes, if your vision is not clear, it will benefit you greatly to pause and consider your objectives. This section outlines material you can start with. By and by, you will be able to come up with definitive objectives for your investment.

Here are some objectives you may work toward by investing in commercial property:

You want to diversify your portfolio

Certainly, you cannot diversify your portfolio if you do not have one already. Thus, this objective is only suitable for those who have been active in real estate investment in some capacity.

With this said, it never hurts to grow and diversify your portfolio as a real estate investor. The more diversified your portfolio is, the better your credentials/reputation is. In addition to diversifying your portfolio, you may be looking to minimize investment risk by investing in a different type of property, which is a smart thing indeed.

Maximizing your income

This one is often the first objective on most peoples' lists. It would make little sense to invest in something if there was no chance of making a profit. If you are indeed trying to maximize returns, what sort of property are you looking to invest in at first? What is the rental return expected? Have you attempted to compare your figures with what similar properties are bringing in?

Growth of capital

If this is one of your objectives, you have to consider the subject of time. How much time do you plan to use up before you hit your preferred monetary figures and what are your figures anyway—how much do you intend to come up with?

Factors That Influence Commercial Property Demand

The reason why some commercial properties seem to have a steady stream of tenants in them while others, no matter how impressive the size and space, go for months without occupants, is because one party paid heed to the factors within this section while the other showed them little regard.

The Location

Location, especially where commercial property is concerned, is everything. If your aim is to rent out your commercial property to a sub-section of tech gurus such as software developers, for example, the most important thing is to ensure your property is in a city or state where that sort of thing has a lot of traction.

Cyclical Demand

Depending on how the economy looks, retail spaces may be in vogue for a spell of time. Other times, tech-office spaces, as well industrial and residential spaces (yes, residential commercial spaces—these days, the millennial generation likes to work, eat, play and live in the same space) will be all the rage.

Market-Driven Value

This alludes to the buyer or tenant's best offer versus that of the seller or property owner. To elaborate, this is not so much of a factor in the case of residential rental property primarily because a residential property owner can tweak rental/sale figures depending on how he likes them. There are times when the market-driven value will be superb and there will be an influx of commercial tenants or prospective buyers. Other times, however, this will not be the case and you may have a lean period.

Shifting Demographics

This is one of the most powerful factors affecting not just the commercial property niche, but also the real estate markets as a whole. You can style your spaces so that they are as attractive to this demographic as possible. You can pick properties to invest in that reflect the rental rates this group of people can afford. You can ensure the internet connectivity is as fast as possible or perhaps fit out the place with throw rugs and floor pillows. The number of things you can do to make your space attracting to millennial run into the millions.

Risks of Investing in Commercial Property

Commercial properties are very different to residential properties; you already know this. With commercial properties, you do stand to pocket higher returns, but quite often, investing in them presents a high risk-high reward scenario.

Economic shifts Influence Commercial properties more than any other property kind

In truth, economic shifts, especially if they are significant, will have an impact on all kinds of real estate. However, the biggest impact tends to be on commercial properties.

Compare this to the residential property market. No matter how badly people want to keep their keep, at the end of the day, they have to sleep somewhere, which means this particular market is not quite as affected.

Area fundamentals may change for the worse

When you are on the lookout for commercial property to invest in, you will want to make sure the place is easy to access and well placed when it comes to transport links. You will also want to make sure that the place is close to other businesses that will, in turn, support the businesses your tenants set up. You will want to keep an eye on how location holds up, which is a smart thing, all factors staying constant.

Zoning changes

Unless your commercial property is one you can easily convert to meet residential use qualities, you may have to sell, prematurely so, your property to a developer for a lower price than you would like, or dig into your pockets and spend heavily on refurbishing the office space so that it meets the standards of a residential space. Both of these choices are not ideal for you in any way or form: you are neither looking to take a loss by being forced to sell your property nor looking to get into residential property via the expensive route of commercial real estate.

The presence of upcoming infrastructure projects

Hold on for a second. Is this not a good thing? Is not the development of retail centers, motorways and train lines a good thing for you as a commercial investor? Surely, these things have a significant impact on people traffic, right?

Well, these things are indeed good things. Such projects are great... but only if they are happening in your area. If the infrastructure projects are happening away from your area, the effect may be very negative for you, with potential tenants drawn to the areas that are experiencing development.

How to Go About Your First Commercial Property Investment

Taking the first step is always the most daunting part especially when it comes buying or investing in something. Here are several steps you can follow to maximize the probability of success with your first commercial property.

A lot of the steps and pointers here mostly call you to apply common sense and pick up as much knowledge as you can.

Visit and look at multiple properties

It is important that you visit as many properties as possible. Nothing beats being on site. You could receive a glowing account of some property from somebody else only to realize it is not quite as hot as the person described it. Likewise, you could get underwhelming accounts of a property only to realize the property is an absolute gem that only needs a personal touch and kitting out.

Look for, and find the experts you will need

As a newbie, you will need some experts to help you out with the oft-complex buying process. The kind of experts required, as well as the requisite number, will rely on the sort of property you are going for.

In truth, there will be a lot of things you can cover on your own, given that you are not too shy of doing a little research and asking a few hard questions, but you may need to hire an expert on many other things as well.

Figure out the state of your finances

Figure out whom to approach for your loan. What banks, home mortgage companies, or credit unions make the most sense to you? Is your local bank a viable option or do their proposed interest rates seem a bit on the silly side? What is your credit score and is it at a place that makes it easier for lenders to consider loaning out to you? What can you do to improve your credit score—if it is in a dire state—so that you become more eligible for a loan? Would the present property owner consider assisting with financing—this is often rare primarily because the property owner does not know you and is more interested in making a buck above everything else; it does happen at times?

Make your offer

It is also smart to go through your lawyer as well. He or she will give you a letter of intent (LOI) that you will need to sign. This letter highlights the basic elements of the transaction. You could download a copy of an LOI from the internet. However, it helps not to be so cheap that you try to bypass the lawyer service—a lawyer will ensure the LOI is not binding in any way so that if you discover flaws in the property before completion of the purchase process, nothing shall bind you to an undesirable property.

Due diligence & escrow

This is the stage where everything gets deathly serious. You are not prospecting anymore: money is about to swap hands. As such, you need to know as much as you can about the property you are looking to buy.

Commercial Real Estate Investment Tips

Here are tips and strategies that will serve you well for a very long time:

Do not be an accumulator of properties; be an investor

The point of investing in something is to be able to turn a profit. Accumulating properties that bring very little by way of income is pointless. Sure enough, Tiny Rowland used to do this and he had quite some success. However, his gung-ho accumulation of properties and assets are perhaps the reason his legacy is not quite as great as it would have otherwise been.

Every commercial property has a lifetime

With time, you will have to revise the state of your property. The roof will need repairs, as will the walls, wallpaper, carpeting, floors, etc. Ensure you have a long-term plan so that your property is always in a competitive state.

Focus on one type of investment at a time

This tip is here to serve a beginner. A time will come when it will be all right to combine as many commercial property types as you like since, at that future point, you will know most of what there is to know about various property types.

Seek a mentor and focus more on his or her mistakes

A mentor will help you make the best decisions moving forward primarily because he or she has been in positions you will find yourself in. This will maximize efficiency, which will help you save the resources of time and money. Even better, mentors will help you notice things you may have otherwise missed.

Chapter 12: Buy and Hold Investment

While purchasing property with the express purpose of holding onto it for an extended period of time is a relatively straightforward process, in order to make the most of this type of investment you are really going to need to become a student of the housing market in your area. This means that while you will still want to constantly be on the lookout for properties, you also need to watch the local housing market and move to purchase a property when the market is in the buyer's favor whenever possible to ensure that each investment you do make will ultimately generate the greatest degree of return on your initial investment possible. When the market is in the sellers' favor on the other hand, then it may be time to reevaluate the current value of any properties you are currently holding on to and sell them if the difference between the price you purchased them at and the one that it would now be possible to sell at have a significant spread.

Regardless of what point the market in your area is currently at, you can rest assured that it is always going to follow the same pattern, you might just need to wait a little while for it to happen. The real estate market cycle is outlined below, remember, it moves in descending order as it is listed and once it reaches the bottom it moves right back to the top once more.

Tipping point: The point at which real estate prices can go no higher, and as such they begin to fall as a result of all of the high prices and new construction that was likely started to take advantage of the climb and the peak. Foreclosures are common during this period as buyers who purchased during the peak and the climb suddenly find themselves owing more on a property than it is currently worth.

Decline: The decline follows the tipping point and is marked by a period of rapidly declining housing prices as additional foreclosures continue to occur. Buyers will be few and far between during this period as many will be fearful of buying a property that is still overvalued. If you have a good idea of what property in your area should be worth, this can be a good time to pick up properties with very little competition.

Bottom: You will know the bottom phase has truly started when you see other investors start to buy back into the market once more. Sellers will be happy to sell for very low prices making deals plentiful and credit and cash flow relatively easy to acquire. It is important to be aware of the timing on this phase if you hope to make the best deals as it typically lasts a shorter period of time than many people assume it will at its onset.

Climb: As the bottom phase continues unabated, prices will slowly start to rise, ending the bottom phase and starting the climb. One the climb phase begins you have a very limited time to make any good deals as inventory will be on the decline once more which means prices are going to start rising and rising quickly.

Peak: Once inventory has decreased significantly and prices have increased in tandem, you will know that you are in the peak phase when prices have reached a point where there is no longer any extra profit to be made. If you are planning on selling, then the peak is the time to do so as it is an absolute seller's market.

Buy and hold success secrets

If you want to be really successful, however, then you are going to want to keep the following tips in mind at all times as well.

Start making money when you buy

While many new investors think that this statement means simply getting a good price on a property, the reality is much more all-inclusive than that. While getting a good price is certainly part of it, it is more about finding other ways to increase value in your direction even more.

Writing up a low offer and getting it occasionally excepted is easy, looking at deals with a broader approach, while difficult, will also be much more rewarding.

Focus on consistent residency

When you are looking for properties, one of your biggest criteria should always be properties that you can expect to quickly and steadily attract tenants or to keep existing tenants for as long as possible. As a buy and hold investor, every month that a property sits empty is a month that you not only lose out on a return on your investment, but have to typically pay out of pocket for property related expenses as well. The best way to get prospective renters in the door is to do what you can to maximize the curb appeal of a given property and the best way to keep them around long term is to look for properties with unique features that are not easily replicated.

Know how involved you want to be from the start

If you are interested in being the person that your tenants call when something goes wrong with the property, then there is virtually no limit to what type of residential real estate that you can invest in.

Create a repeatable process

As you are going about finding your first rental property, you are going to want to keep in mind the ways you went about doing so that worked, as well as those that didn't so that you can repeat the successful steps next time and save yourself lots of wasted effort, and possibly some time as well. This same mentality should then be used throughout the buying, renovating and renting process.

Finding the right property

When it comes to actually getting started implementing a buy and hold strategy, finding the right property is half the battle in and of itself. If you are looking to get your first round of tenants into a property as quickly as possible, then that means you are going to want to look for properties that appear as though they will require relatively little work besides updating the kitchen and the bathroom and maybe throwing down some new carpet. Aside from that, what you are going to want to be most aware of is what type of target audience a given area is likely to attract based on the amenities that it offers and the average rental rate for the area in question.

Know your audience

Regardless of what the amenities in a given area are like, it is important that you pinpoint them early on as the characteristics of a good property are going to change based on who you can realistically expect to want to live there. Ensuring you only go into the hunt after you know what type of renters an area is going to attract means that you won't need to worry about working against the property that you buy and can instead focus on enhancing its attractiveness in a specific way.

Consider the costs

When it comes to finding the right area to practice the buy and hold strategy in, it is important to keep in mind what other rentals in the area are renting for and also what the property tax rate in the area is like. The amount that you will be required to pay for property taxes can vary dramatically, even over a relatively small area which means a deal that might be manageable in one neighborhood might not be tenable just one neighborhood over. Additionally, you will want to take into account how many other available rental properties there are in a given area and what, if any, distinguishing features a property that you have your eye on has to make it worth more or less than the going rate.

Look to the future

Finally, when it comes to determining what area you are interested in looking for rental property deals in, then it is important to always judge an area with an eye to the future as well. As the name implies, a good buy and hold strategy is long term which means that a given area has the potential to change considerably, affecting your investment in one way or another.

Paying for your first buy and hold investment

After you have found the perfect property to buy and hold, the next thing you are going to need to do is to worry about paying for it. First and foremost, mortgage insurance doesn't apply to buy and hold properties so if you are planning on going to a traditional financial institution for a loan then you are going to need to bring at least 20 percent of the total price of the property with you. If you don't have this much capital to put down on the property you can instead consider getting a pair of mortgages instead which will make securing a profitable rental agreement much more difficult than it might otherwise be.

Rather than going to a traditional financial establishment, a better choice if you are planning to make a habit of buying and holding multiple properties is to seek out a direct lender to form a mutually beneficial relationship with. Fostering this relationship will likely ultimately lead to better fees, small down payments and an all-around better loan that will make it easier for you to profit from new properties in the long run. When it comes to finding the right lender to work with you are going to want to consider the number of other investors they are currently working with, the number of loans you would be allowed to have outstanding at a single time and the types of property that they are most comfortable working with.

Chapter 13: Investing in REITs

REITs stand for Real Estate Investment Trusts and are one of the most straight-forward ways in which you can invest in real estate. The logic behind REITs rests in a provision set forth by the federal government. REITs pay no federal income tax, so long as they're paying out at least 90% of their profits in the form of dividends to shareholders. REITs can allow you to get a piece of the action on big properties, such as hotels, malls, vacation properties, parking garages, and commercial high rises.

The formation of REITs was undertaken in an effort to strengthen the middle class by providing more high value opportunities for private investors of moderate wealth. Congress passed the Real Estate Investment Trust Act of 1960, which was intended to create a compelling tax incentive for individuals to form investment pools that would ultimately benefit the average American investor. Originally, there were restrictions placed upon these investment pools, namely that the properties owned by the pools had to hire a property management and property leasing service to run the property. In 1986, with the passage of the Tax Reform Act, these restrictions were removed. Later, in 1999, the REIT Modernization Act was passed (and it's still in effect as of 2015) allowing REITs to form taxable REIT subsidiaries (TRS's) to perform services for tenants. It was the REIT Modernization Act that brought the dividend distribution amount down to 90% from its previous 95%.

Investing in REITs is very similar to investing in stocks, and choosing the right REIT is similar to the process of choosing the right stock. You can rely on standard trading platforms, such as those operated by Scott Trade and E*Trade to help you shop and choose a good REIT.

A final note on REITs: like stocks, but unlike other property investments, REITs are highly liquid. You don't need to wait through the tenuous process of selling an entire property to get your money out. In most cases you can easily sell your share in an REIT just as you would a stock or bond.

Smart Investing—Never Use Your Own Name

Another nice thing about REITs is that technically you're buying a share in a pool and the REIT, not you, is the principle owner of the property or properties. When you purchase an investment property on your own, you also try to avoid having the property listed in your own name.

Instead, you should look into setting up an LLC (Limited Liability Company) and using it to manage your properties.

The problem with running your properties on your own, as a sole proprietor, is that you're fully liable for damages in excess of what's covered by your property insurance. If someone gets injured on your property and they exhaust your coverage limits, then you'll be personally liable for any further damages. This has led to the bankruptcy of more than a few investors. The hoops you have to go through to set up an LLC really aren't that cumbersome or expensive (a few hundred dollars, or a few thousand if you use an attorney). Since the filing requirements aren't that messy, a lot of real estate investors set up separate LLC's for each property (or property group) that they invest in. That way, if something goes wrong with one property, it can be put into bankruptcy and the other LLC's won't be affected.

Chapter 14: Tips for Success

Here are some additional tips for succeeding at investing in real estate:

Start Small

Investors who have had a good amount of success began small. They buy one property to start. Before they purchased, they researched the area where they decided they wanted to invest. The ideals that make a good location to invest in -shopping convenience, schools, adjacency to major highways/freeways, businesses that provide services to the residents in the area. There is information from a number of sources that can provide the data you can use to get all the information needed.

Start making money when you buy

While many new investors think that this statement means simply getting a good price on a real estate property, the reality is much more all-inclusive than that.

While getting a good price for a piece of real estate is certainly part of it, it is more about finding other ways you can get immediately increase the value from your real estate investment.

Focus on consistent residency

When you are looking for real estate properties, one of your biggest criteria should always be properties that you can expect to quickly and steadily attract tenants or to keep existing tenants for as long as possible.

Keep this in mind, as a buying and holding real estate investor, every month that a property sits empty is a month that you not only lose out on a profit on your investment but you actually have to pay out of pocket for property related expenses as well.

Know how involved you want to be from the start

If you are interested in being the person that your tenants always contact when something goes wrong with the property, then there is virtually no limit to what type of residential real estate you can invest in.

If, however, you are hoping for something a little "more hands off," then what you are instead going to want to consider is using a property management company for all your day to day landlord issues and duties.

Forging and Fostering Important Relationships

Relationships with other real estate investors can be forged online or locally. A quick google search will take you to vibrant online communities such as the biggerpockets.com website where enthusiastic discussions can be found on a variety of topics related to property investment. You can also find active discussions on investment strategy and opportunities on the professional social networking site, Linked-In.

Investment Location

The property you plan to invest in needs to be in a good location. This is probably the most important part of real estate investing. Finances and employment are other essentials that need to be part of the research to find areas that demonstrate they are stable and profitable. Affordability, population growth, and job growth are three considerations that will influence your decision where the best places are for investing and creating positive cash flow.

Don't plan while viewing a property

If you find yourself making a plan regarding what you would do with a potential real estate property then simply stop planning.

What you want to do is make sure to do some research on the local area and real estate market before making any plans to purchase real estate property.

If you don't do any research on the local area or real estate market when viewing a property for the first time, then you will have left yourself at a huge disadvantage when it comes to determining the right price to offer for the property.

Don't expect too much too soon

While you can realistically rent out a property in certain states in a matter of days, this is certainly the exception, not the rule.

As such, having an unrealistic time frame of how long it is going to be before your new real estate investment starts to turn a profit is crucial to being prepared both mentally and financially.

What' s more, the process of renting out a property can easily take much longer than expected, simply due to unexpected external factors that cropped up after you were already in the process of trying to turn a profit on the property.

Don't overestimate your abilities

However, when it comes to investing in real estate, it is important to have a more "realistic view of yourself and the immediate success you will have.

Simply, to save time and money when it comes to investing in real estate you want to make sure to do a lot of research and to slowly and patiently go about the process of purchasing your first real estate property.

Specifically, this applies most frequently to new real estate investors who overestimate their personal ability to undertake or complete renovations in a timely manner on a given property.

Don't underestimate relationships

When it comes to successfully investing and succeeding in real estate it is important to keep in mind that even the most self-sufficient real estate investor is going to need to foster a few key relationships if they hope to be successful in the long run.

First and foremost, you are going to want to find a real estate agent that you can work with who you trust to find you the best real estate deals possible.

Conclusion

Whether your intent is to fulfill your dreams of owning a place of your own or to secure sound investments that will give you a comfortable nest egg on which to retire, if you follow the advice in this book, you'll be well on your way to becoming a successful property owner with a steady stream of passive income at your disposal.

Owning an investment property sometimes calls for decisions to be made that are difficult to make, but need to be made because they affect how you manage your investment, or if the property begins to drain your finances, produce a negative cash flow. You need to know when to let go.

The purpose of your investing in a real estate property was to create a steady, positive cash flow income. The change in the neighborhood could very possibly change the income from positive to negative.

Knowing what your profits and losses are will help you decide how long you can, or wish to continue on a loss cycle. Trying to play catch up financially if you allow the deficit to continue is not a great way to handle the situation.

Rather than continuing to hold on to the property, it may be a good idea to get out while you financially can.

Preparing for unexpected expenses before you purchase your real estate investment will help you understand all the fees involved with the purchase transaction and be able to make the process move along as quickly and smoothly as possible.

When you understand that repairs and maintenance costs for your property are an ownership reality, considering the options of estimating the annual costs and which one feels the best option to go with can alleviate a great number of financial problems in the future. The key towards successfully purchasing future investments is through proper planning and preparation. You need to be disciplined enough to calculate how much you need to save and then actually start saving from your income sources right away.

There is really no greater return on investment with reduced risk than real estate. If you properly analyze and strategize the best way to invest in real estate, you will be able to receive a monthly income and have a profit left over after paying your mortgage and other expenses.

Make sure you do ample amount of planning and strategizing so you can reduce your risk and get the highest return from your investment.

As you start investing in properties, you are bound to make some mistakes on the way. However, what you want to do is learn from these mistakes. Never let failure bring you down. If you keep working hard, you will gain experience and eventually become a wise real estate investor.

Learning real estate can be like learning a new language for some people, but we never knew how to speak when we grew up, but then practice happened. Hence, training, learning, and experience will help you become a better investor. You have to focus on the learning procedure of investing and, eventually, you will master it!